Wakefield Press

Live at Mr Jake's

Steve Brock published his first collection of poetry *The Night is a Dying Dog* (Friendly Street/ Wakefield Press) in 2007, and received a grant from Arts South Australia for the completion of *Double Glaze*, published by Five Islands Press in 2013. He is the co-translator with Sergio Holas and Juan Garrido-Salgado of *Poetry of the Earth: Mapuche Trilingual Anthology* (Interactive Press, 2014). Steve completed a PhD in Australian literature at Flinders University in 2003. His work has featured in *Best Australian Poems* (Black Inc.) and has been published in journals in Australia and overseas. His most recent collection is the chapbook *Jardin du Luxembourg* (Garron Publishing, 2016). Steve was a featured writer at Adelaide Writers' Week in 2017.

Also by Steve Brock

The Night is a Dying Dog
Double Glaze
Jardin du Luxembourg

Live at Mr Jake's

Steve Brock

Wakefield Press

Wakefield Press
16 Rose Street
Mile End
South Australia 5031
www.wakefieldpress.com.au

First published 2020

Cover designed by Liz Nicholson, Wakefield Press
Cover illustration by Peter Doley
Edited by Graham Rowlands
Text designed and typeset by Michael Deves, Wakefield Press

ISBN 978 1 74305 710 0

NATIONAL
LIBRARY
OF AUSTRALIA

A catalogue record for this
book is available from the
National Library of Australia

For my father

Contents

Section One

Jardin du Luxembourg

walking around the Jardin du Luxembourg
on our way back to the hotel
we stumble across a film set
the camera
set up on light rails
ridden by a man in a hat
coat and scarf
with long hair
who looks vaguely familiar

a young, bearded director
walks around holding a megaphone
and consults
with assistants
while crew members
fend off onlookers
by stringing tape tree to tree

someone counts to three
in French
and closes the clapper board

we watch as policemen
in blue uniforms and caps
walk diagonally
across the evenly spaced
chestnut groves
blowing their whistles

and moving on
imaginary bystanders

while a man in a 1920s
grey coloured suit
holding a fedora hat
in his right hand
strides purposefully
as though oblivious
to the action around him

the director calls cut
and it's only then
I realise that a man reading a newspaper
and a woman in a long dress
with a summer umbrella
sitting on a bench in the background
are part of the scene
as they get up and walk towards us

after some consultation
with the director
the next scene
moves away from the trees
closer to the path
where we are standing

instead of the camera
running along the rails
it stays fixed

and the main actor
rehearses his walk
taking advice from an assistant

he now walks away from the camera
right hand still holding his fedora
his face now closer
looks like an ageing Alain Delon
expression fixed and focused
oblivious to crew and onlookers

maybe he's a big star
of French cinema
he stares at us and through us and beyond us
his walk is slightly exaggerated
raising his knees a little higher
and taking slightly larger steps
than he might do in real life
but like a face in makeup
one can imagine
his walk will translate perfectly on screen
a romantic walk
that will resonate with European cinema
and signal a certain class and attitude

I wonder if he walks
with this poise and strength
through his own life
with a face not easily subject to distraction
perhaps the walk and face

are integral to the success of his career
unlike my own uncertain gait
hobbled by work injury
and a visage that lacks confidence generally

or never was appropriately attuned
to other lives
'protagonist disease' my daughter tells me
a failure to recognise
you are someone sitting on set
in the background of another individual's reality
a bit player

it's not clear though
what this man's role is
perhaps only a bit part himself
something that like his career
might get scrapped

or maybe he's the plain clothes detective
the star of the film
close to solving the case

or has he committed some kind of crime
and his walk is a confidence trick
as he hides in plain sight?

the take begins again
and just as the man
nears the end of his walk
an elderly female tourist

ducks under the tape
and crosses the set
to cries of disbelief from the director

the actors break character
one of the police walking past us
smiles and mutters *très bon*!
so that we feel we're part
of the action at last

and indeed as the police walk by
in several re-takes
they rap off the onlookers
pointing and moving us on
which we do eventually
as the weather cools slightly
and the tedium of movie making
results in tired legs

2

the next day
I think I see the character
in the same suit
walking in a slightly exaggerated way
down the steps of Notre Dame

I look twice but it's just
another local
so people really do walk this way in Paris?

since my arrival
I've been consciously walking in the steps
of my literary heroes
Cortázar mainly
I recognise Boulevard Saint-Michel
and Boulevard Saint-Germain
from his novels
and the Polidor restaurant . . .

Hem, Rimbaud, Baudelaire
the real difficulty would be walking
where no famous writer
artist or philosopher
hadn't walked before

Cortázar himself
was known to close his eyes
put his finger on a map of Paris
and go wherever it landed

I was probably closest to Cortázar
while lost
off Boulevard Saint-Germain
discovering old cobble stoned streets
we wouldn't be able to find again

mostly our role here
is confined to that of tourist
as much as we try and walk like locals
we get tripped
by cultural faux pas and mis-readings

we even go on a walking tour
a literary one
which takes us to the apartment
where Joyce finished *Ulysses*
Hem's residence
when he first moved to Paris
and his studio around the corner
in the same building where Verlaine lived
now home to the Verlaine Café
ending up via Orwell
on the steps of the church
which was the setting for *Les Misérables*

and as our guide
takes us through the scene
where Jean Valjean gives generous alms
to beggars
he is approached
by present-day beggars
still playing out the same role
like any church in Europe
testing our commitment
to Christian stories

like in the Gare de Lyon station
where an old man
approaches the Starbucks coffee queue
and I put one euro
in his cup
and he clasps my hand

in the rough palms
of his two hands
and stutters a heart-felt blessing
only the poor can give
and I think of Christ
and Che
getting close to the lepers
while I eat my croissant
with my left hand
taking a few bites
before they announce our train
and we join the others
with tickets to somewhere

3

we find new folds in Paris
in the company of Chris
whom we meet at the Fontaine Saint-Michel
and go for dinner
not far from the Beat Hotel

Chris directs the waiters
in commanding French
as he tells us about his publisher in Paris
and the research for a new novel

I ask him how he feels
about the whole Napoleonic/Pantheon thing
walking in the steps of the big writers
and history makers

he says you can let it stifle you
or look at it like
see what's possible
see what can be achieved

and maybe that's easier to do
as an Australian
or someone from the new world
as growing up around all this history
it would be easy to say why bother

Chris walks us back to our hotel
and I feel my stride expand
my knees rise a little a higher
after all we're in Paris!
think of the possibilities!

Paris – a conqueror's guide

writers and philosophers
enthroned in the Pantheon
statues of Napoleon
his arches of triumph
scenes of Napoleonic victory
it's enough to make you want to
conquer Europe
and after a kilo of raw beef
at the Polidor
I feel I probably could
but it's the small victories
in which we find solace
like locating the side entrance to the Louvre
and dodging the tremendous queue
or skipping the lines
at the Musée Rodin
and Musée d'Orsay
with our museum pass
or making it to the top of the Eiffel Tower
and back
without being pick pocketed
or successfully ordering
two bottles of water
in French
from the local kiosk
or dragging a couple of green chairs
around the Jardin du Luxembourg

where we find some Parisian sun
and I day dream of Cortázar
we share the spoils
of the day's victories
with a kid who sleeps
on the corner of Boulevard Saint-Michel
and Rue Cujas
with a well groomed dog
and three different brands
of dog biscuits
mouths open to the night air
and finally
squeezing enough bandwidth
out of the hotel wifi
to upload our daily triumphs
to our legions of followers
on Facebook.

LA

LA is a lonely city
the B-grade actor
tells me
at the bar
of the San Remo Hotel
on North Beach
San Francisco

and he kind of confirms it
by not answering my call
when I arrive

I'm trying to pick the barman
who served Bukowski
at the Musso & Frank Grill
on Hollywood Boulevard
when it hits me

maybe it's the wine
catching up

the red booths here in rows
with waiters
in red jackets
running up and down
either side of me

the yellow glow
of the lights
on the walls

I feel a sense of speed
rise inside me
as though I'm racing toward
the mahogany panel
two booths ahead

and I realise
I'm in a Mondrian painting

I guess this city is fast too.

The Hollywood Hotel

an inventory
of items
in my room:

a compact black umbrella
purchased in heavy rain
from a street seller
in New York

poetry books
by Cortázar, Alejandro Murguía
and Mayakovsky
bought at City Lights Books
and two copies
of Roberto Vargas'
Nicaragua, yo te canto besos, balas y sueños de libertad
discovered in a second hand bookstore

a 1974 retro Ed Dorn original
picked up at Bolerium Books
in the Mission District

one ticket to the Beat Museum
given to me
by a bit actor from LA

a serviette
from the Frolic Room
with a poem

written in block letters
in blue pen
by the barfly
Tony de la Paz

a couple of empty
bottles of Sierra Nevada
Pale Ale

a ticket stub
from the wash and fold
on the Upper West Side
with Geoff Goodfellow's name on it

a collection of dimes and quarters
and other change
I haven't got my head around

and the *Gary Snyder Reader*
I carried with me from Australia
reminding me about roots
and the need to plant seeds
upon my return home.

Presence

I walk by a house
each morning
its white Corinthian pillars
overlook a park and creek
with a view to low lying hills
in the south
where the sky is still coloured
from the dawn
an elderly western woman
sits on the front steps
in a kimono
smoking a cigarette
and drinking coffee
there's something about her presence
which inflects the landscape
with a sense of tragedy
I don't turn to say hello
but rather let myself become absorbed
into her landscape of contemplation

Barcelona

Carrer de la Princesa
en el Born
is an open wound
that runs through our dreams
shouts and taconeos
of passers by
the bark of dogs
echo through our apartment
a kind of cajón flamenco drum
where my inner thoughts sound

I feel we have a good handle on Spain
flamenco in a baroque bar
with 17th century walls
and jugs of sangria
paella in the Restaurante Salamanca
beneath a roof of cured hams
a plate of cured ham and cheese
with a half bottle of El Coto de Rioja
long afternoons of tapas
with copas de cerveza
Gaudi's Sagrada Familia and Casa Batlló
Picasso street views
from our apartment balcony
on the fifth floor
where across the street
in a lit window

a Renoir crosses her legs
and uncrosses them

I get the feeling
since arriving in Europe
I'm finally arriving at the subject
Lorca's cante jondo
street artists and a language
we can decode
re-united with long-lost family
we feel at home.

The commuter

there's an office worker
I've seen on the train
these past few years
he's maybe ten years younger
non-descript features

that somehow evoke
a friend from my youth
so that whenever I see him
there's a flicker of recognition
inside me
arising from the coals
of a friendship 20 years past

and while we cross paths daily
he rarely crosses my mind
until this evening
when I unfold the local rag
and recognise him on page 4

the photo taken from a low angle
giving him a new stature
caught mid-stride
oblivious to the executor of the image
eyes slightly raised
toward some higher purpose
face business-like
dead-pan as always

he towers above the word
COMMUTE
writ large in Times New Roman

as though he could be
a Greek God
Achilles perhaps
returning from battle
having slain Hector
to avenge the death
of his beloved comrade
Patroclus

receiving news
from the front
through white, ceramic
headphones

and I'm proud to claim him
as one of my tribe

after all
we go back a long way
on the 5.18 pm
of the Seaford line.

Live at Mr Jake's

Saturday night
a kid balls the wall
as Pete cues up
his recording software
He'll tire soon
I read the first poem
and we're halfway through
when a possum
jumps on the roof
we start again
and there's a buzzing
around the light
A blowie?
No, a bee
I catch them all the time
Pete produces a plastic
take-away container
as I eye the clock
and in one swift motion
expertly swoops up the bee
and takes it outside
a small victory
against Monsanto
we resume the recording
and Mr Jake
makes his entrance
sniffs the bell of the sax

with the no. 2 reed
but like a seasoned studio cat
pads around silently
as we continue the take
then there's a knock at the door
Sharon appears
Pete laments
our long list of intruders
and she gives him a kiss
while behind the mic
I meditate on the poem
as anti-poem
lines buckling under the weight of all
we're not letting in
and I want to open it up to the multitudes
turn it into a big-boned meandering thing
of improbable parentage
larger than life
like Mr Jake

Experimental

Ouyang Yu
invites me to comment
on a thread
about experimental poetry

ah I think u r scared
he writes

the thread includes an experimental poem
featuring a white jump suit
with genitals

I think of *Saturday Night Fever*
and images of clothes in poems
Mayakovsky's cloud in trousers
the borrowed warmth
of Ted Berrigan's jacket
Schuyler's loose jeans
he wears like a life
Bolton's art critic coat
with an extra arm
Bolaño's white overalls

until experimental appears
like another garish shirt
worn by a poet you'd like to meet
at a 70s retro party
only you're too stoned
to know it's dress up

and wonder when you got so out of touch
with fashion
but it's small surprise
as you don't get out much anymore
and you'd check with the host to be sure
but you're too scared to ask

Seminal poem

R just got her PhD
but her examiner
chided her
for using the word seminal
in her exegesis
as it derived
from the word semen.
Come again?
And the metaphor
of the bouquet
in one of her poems
was heteronormative.
I suggested the root word
of seminal
was seed
but recommended
she consult
the etymology of the word.
D asked
what if the bouquet
was for a gay marriage?

K left to get a kebab
and later at the reading
I expounded on the parallels
between the humble kebab
and poetry

the bite sized strophes
strung together
with something sharp
but she drifted off
and missed the crux
of my argument

the takeaway being
it was time for another wine.

Dreaming with Ted Berrigan

I met Ted Berrigan
in a dream

wearing a T-shirt
standing in a sparsely
furnished room

the early Berrigan
not yet bed ridden
but distinctly
pot bellied

& the beard
of course

it was a vivid dream
I can't remember
if he said anything
literary

but he seemed pleased
to be there

Sparrows

a flock of sparrows
fly toward my fourth-floor window;
as they get closer
I see they're only
autumn leaves
in a gust of wind

later the sparrows
revisit me in my dream;
only now they are sparrows
for real

Section Two

In office

Monday morning
after a month's leave
and travel overseas
the veins of winter leaves
on the wet pavement
are the fine bones of an animal
preserved in the period
of a former self.

I think of lines by Paul Celan

our apartment in Barcelona
keeps me awake at night
I think of Paul Celan
complaining in his letters
about living above an intersection
in an apartment in Paris
the noise drove him mad
and he feared the impact
on his writing

reading his letters
I thought I'd love to live
in a noisy apartment
in Paris
now I see how it could get to you

I used to worry about the distant hum
of freeway traffic
but returning home from Europe
it mostly sounds peaceful here
the birds and wind in the trees

I get my bearings again
from the stars
of which I only saw a few
in Europe
while lining up for tickets
to the Alhambra

it seems a small miracle
just to be able to make your own coffee
and reach into the fridge
for juice and yoghurt
I'm a man with a fruit bowl again
I make toast
and mess up the kitchen
late into the evening

in my dream
there is something soft
against my bare foot
she gently bites
drawing me out
into feline consciousness

haven't slept
with a cat on my bed
for three weeks.
I wake up happy.

The window

I wake up
in the middle of the night
in a panic

about my dead-end job
the credit card
the housing market

until poetry appears
like a window
I go through
& compose
a couple of works
of genius

by daylight
they won't be much
of course

but it's enough
to get me
through the night

You only queue twice

standing on the Puente Romano
in Cordoba
watching the rio Guadalquivir
run beneath
like time itself
I do the math
2000 divided by 44 = 45
history is nothing more than this
45 times a life of error and uncertainty
the main lesson of monuments in Europe
for which you only queue twice
unless you want the audio guide too
but mostly we take the negative capability option
in the face of poor signage or poor French
and let our consciousness run freely
against the object
sounding it out
although sometimes I feel a need
for an audio-guide to life
an authoritative voice
with a haughty accent
telling us how magnificent it all is
and not to expect too much
from the vaguely unsatisfactory present
I guess that's what literature is
one never-ending guidebook

with tips from those
who've done it all before
and our own collisions
with objects and texts
give us something to say uniquely
and which one might call poetry
while I won't be leaving
any monuments
and have conquered little
beyond a 700 square metre block
in an outer suburb
I hope these notes might
help the next person.

Some mornings

I get so bored
with myself and poetry
all I'm going to write about
is me standing in front of a mirror
my dumb nakedness in the half light
of a small room where my wife sleeps
I do up the buttons
on my shirt
one
by
one
my left thumb
still smarting
from the steam iron.

The dust settles

there are no messages
on Gmail
Facebook
Messenger
Instagram
no-one calls
I spend the afternoons
sleeping off the week
sleeping off the wine
and feel myself
come back down
to ground zero
having to start again
just the blank page
an empty sky
no new job openings
no publishing opportunities
no new poems
no reading invites
no launches
the mind is quiet
life doesn't owe me anything
Monday morning
I watch
as the pedestrian crossing
counts down
another 22 seconds
of my life.

On being

it's the person
I didn't meet
at the café
the ticket
with the winning prize
unfound
in her handbag
the philosopher
a friend recommended
in a pub
in my twenties
that I didn't get on to
until my forties
and then lost
on the chapter
of death and dying
the poets
that remain unread
and undiscovered
the unwritten
the ideas
that escaped me
the ones
I didn't
get out of bed for
the ones

I got into bed for
the girl I left waiting
on a street corner
in Buenos Aires
for a soccer match
did she even turn up?
the articles
I didn't find time to write
the children
unborn
the calls
I didn't make
to loved ones
dying
the stranger's hand
un-shook
the kiss
left hanging
on a cold moon
of my youth
it's the lives
unlived
that make mine.

Animal poetics

a puppy attached to a pram
jumps around and bites the lead
making a game of it
to mum's frustration
he turns his attention to a long piece of bark
picks it up from the side of the path
and carries it along in his mouth
shaking his head until it drops.
I watch as they take a separate path
until I shake my imagination free
and move to the next distraction.

Section Three

New Years Eve 2010

1
we ushered in the New Year
talking about 2012

he told me
2012 was the end of a 5,000 year
Mayan cycle
that would bring
a new consciousness
for humankind
telepathy for example ...

2
I didn't tell him
I'd already
blown open my consciousness
back in 1995
in the far north of Chile
where the San Pedro cactus
grows freely
in neatly manicured front gardens

after drinking all night
with locals
we lopped off
a couple of thick branches
with a machete

on our way back
to the house
we came across
the Firefly

how dare you pass
without saluting the Firefly!

what part of the infinity
do you come from?

his eyes wide & vacant
a dark, tattooed hand
grasped my hand

he drew his words out
like a cool breeze

his tattooed chest
open to the dawn

& from under his armpit
he pulled a great sandwich

he wasn't the kind of guy
to refuse hospitality

each one of us
took a bite

before the Firefly
returned to his orbit

3
across the dirt road
from the house
en la población
was a store
called Don Juanito
on my third visit
that day
hands & face blackened
asking for another bag of coal
Don Juanito exclaimed
that must be some fucking cow
you've got there!

we boiled the cactus
in the back yard
for eight hours
before draining the juice
through a stocking

4
above my left eye
a wall broke away
a gaping hole appeared
which grew to about
a third of my forehead

I had access
to an infinite array of images
& travelled through my mind

opening windows
colourful & organic

witness to scenes
of thought & emotion
with colours, shapes & memories
combining to create
facets of my character

I travelled at high speed
through orange, green & purple
landscapes of mind
I could create any image at will
& images were generating themselves
in pure, free thought

speech & sentences
appeared to me
as blocks of meaning

conversation
was the building of a wall
between neighbours
brick by brick

5
in 2010
I was happy
to sip Pisco
on ice
without the need
for fireworks.

Day burner

I've got this friend
who always seems to have
a lot of time on his hands

I'm not sure how he pays the bills
but every so often
he drives in
from interstate
in a station wagon
and in the back
are small boxes
all shapes and sizes
full of speaker components
and musical instruments

he stays with us
for a few days
while he drives around town
visiting burnt out DJs
and old rockers
with long hair and earrings
grey and balding on top
and they sense that like them
he has a lot of time on his hands
and they spend a couple of hours
talking about their problems
before agreeing to buy

half a dozen needles
at 100 dollars a pop

which my mate bought
at 10 dollars a pop
from a supplier in China
who sourced them from a jail somewhere
where some poor bastard
makes these things by hand
and if he doesn't make his quota
of 500 a day
they'll spray him with pepper spray
and put him in solitary
for 30 days
waking him every 20 minutes
with bursts of heavy metal music

and at the end of the day
my friend will pick me up
and complain there's too many
trucks on the road
and how there should be one road for trucks
and one for cars
and he's rung the transport department
and gotten on to someone
who senses this is a guy
with a lot of time on his hands
which is always dangerous in politics
so they go into some detail
about how there was a plan

to build a separate road for trucks
but this was dependent
on another plan
to share the profits from the mining boom
until along came a little thing
called the GFC
and the mine didn't get dug

another time
he became obsessed
with street lights
left on during the day
'day burners'
he called them

he created his own web page
for people to report
lights left on during the day
and at one stage
considered standing
for the Greens

it's surprising though
how many lights
are left on during the day

when I opened the front door
this morning
I saw my outside
light was left on

instead of telling myself
'I've left the light on'
I thought
'aah, a day burner'

and knew that something
far more sinister
was afoot.

Good Friday

I bit into a small chocolate egg
and got a toothache
the day before Good Friday

I rang my dentist
but they were booked out
and would be closed
over the Easter weekend
I dropped some painkillers
and hoped for the best

I rose on Good Friday
still in pain
and called a number
I found online
for emergency dental work
a dentist answered

I've got a sore tooth

I can take a look at it
but it will cost you a little more
than your ordinary dentist

like how much more?

depends on what I do
if I just pull the tooth say
or have to cut out a nerve

hang on, I think I might just need a filling
how much would that cost?

around $480
and if I have to take an x-ray
or if I find anything else
it may be more

OK, I might just wait it out

I hung up
the tooth hurt a whole lot less

I turned on the TV
and saw on the news
pubs and hotels
were serving alcohol
on Good Friday
in Adelaide
for the first time
in 100 years

my wife went down to our local
and picked up a six pack
of Golden Ale

two beers later
the pain was gone.

Taxi driver

the taxi driver
with a thick Russian accent
and fur trapper hat
tells me we're on the brink
of financial ruin
the banks
in the US
printing more and more money
85 billion a day

I only need to go a few blocks
to escape the Melbourne weather
the fare comes to $6.45
I hand him my credit card
and tell him
make it an even ten

where's that coming from?
he cries
and hands me back the receipt
for $6.45

I fold it up
and put it in my pocket

like a prayer
for real economics.

A blessing

a guy asks me for some change
to buy a yiros
on Rundle St
he had a neatly
packed army bag
and aviator shades
his clothes seemed clean
but I could see the want
coming through
three day growth
in his cheeks
I was going
to walk on
but felt
a sudden empathy
for a hustler
on the road
and there was a fiver
loose in my back pocket
as I'd locked
myself out of the house
without my wallet
and had borrowed
cash
from my mother
I was looking to spend

the fiver
on a coffee
down the east end
but this guy's want
seemed greater than mine
whether for food
drink or something else
so I paused
and reached in to my back pocket
and passed him the clean note
and he cried out
to the street
Bless you! Bless you sir!
which made me smile.

Juliaca Station, Peru

the train
from Cuzco
had a long stopover
at Juliaca station

we asked
a friendly Peruvian couple
to mind our seats
and stepped off
into the warm night air

away from the platform
and street sellers
among the shadows
of empty carriages
we smoked a couple of blunts

two Quechua women
emerged from the darkness

their faces
two frightened moons
in the night

we motioned
it was safe
to cross
and watched
as they ran along the tracks
and jumped the train

the great loads on their backs
wobbling beneath
colourful blankets

Glass

once I was fascinated
by window cleaners
working many storeys high

now they come past
my multistorey window
and I barely notice their faces
unshaven and grimacing

stuck to my screen
half a metre away
I'm vaguely aware
of the noise
of clanging chains
and rails
as they work
past my window
and overhear people
in work stations nearby
ask each other
to repeat themselves

suddenly
the quiet
of a view
over Victoria Square
behind clean glass.

Personality test

a colleague
shows me the results
of his psychometric testing

it cost the company
a couple of grand

he had to work
in groups
through different
scenarios

the test went for the full day
& they had different individuals
observing each exercise
to avoid prejudice

the report was detailed
with complex graphs
mapping his leadership qualities
his emotional resilience
his problem solving abilities
his communication skills

the fact he liked to be in control
of situations
& was good
at small talk

it took some time to read
& I kept looking
but still couldn't find it

apparently they failed to pick up
he's a dickhead.

American homo

we take a cab
off Times Square
back to the hotel
on the Upper West Side

the Bangladeshi driver
tells us how New York
is being saved
by gay marriage

people are coming
from around the country
to marry
and lift the economy
in the process

he turns around
to the back seat
and looks me in the eye
are you homo?

I shake my head
it's just like the city
of Sodom and Gomorrah
he explains

on this point
I enquire if gay marriage
far from saving the city
might lead to its destruction

he quotes a passage from the bible
where God says
he will no longer destroy
the cities of men

will the gays go to heaven or hell?
I ask

he's a practising Muslim
and prays five times a day
has a wife and three children
and lives a moral life
he will go to heaven
while the homos
will burn in hellfire

we pull up
outside the Milburn Hotel
and as my mate
places some bills
in the driver's hand
he looks him squarely in the eye

Are you homo?

Section Four

Still life

writing poetry
is like a bowl of lemons
in morning light
on the kitchen table
you need the optimism
of the lemon
the certainty of style
and form
and the ability
to lend yourself
like the humble lemon
to season other parts
of your life
to go with family
and work
until one day
you have enough lemons
to live off alone

Bird man

I was a boy of ten
staying in the country
with my auntie and cousins
for the summer school holidays

we were going crabbing
and shot half a dozen galahs
with a .22 rifle
to use as bait

as my auntie stacked them
in the freezer
wrapped in plastic
she cautioned me:
you better not tell your father

twelve years ago
my auntie died of breast cancer

on the anniversary
of her death
I sit in the coronary care unit
in a darkened room
listening to my father
gasp for breath

galahs stacked in rows
in the freezer of my mind.

Filling up

I hang up the nozzle
and pour water
under the fuel cap
to wash off any residue

an old girlfriend
taught me this
in my teens

I don't know
why I persist

she died some years ago
and the white duco
of this 20-year-old car
shows no sign of rust

you should've seen her smile
heard her laugh
a rare thing

I pour again
and watch the water
run over it

The kind of friend

you hear some slide guitar
and want to share it with him
or a novel you've read
but it's been at least a year
since you last phoned
or swapped books
and the names in conversations
have become unfamiliar
and if you don't ring now
you'll ring tomorrow.

On the passing of a friend

you asked me how I felt about it
only a few weeks after the event
at that time I didn't know how to feel
it was certainly not how society
would've expected me to feel
in a Hallmark card kind of way

more like a man travelling on a train
and there's another man waiting on a platform
so you have a slightly different
sense of space/time
consistent with Einstein's theorem
I would then get off the train
and cry for no reason
which made me think maybe
his death had affected me more than I let on
but it was still somewhere ahead of me
so I would see his likeness in a crowd

when we spoke about death like this
it reminded me of when we were teenagers
and we would share our most intimate thoughts
like the way we imagined a Wednesday to be blue
and Tuesday to be yellow
Monday a kind of laminated white
that's where my feeling about death resided
somewhere before and after language

now his daughter comes and learns piano
from my daughter every Saturday afternoon
I sit and talk with his widow
we sift through various aspects of his life
as though trying to find some kind of clue
or something we could remedy
while in the background
his girl runs through her scales

My friend the poet

for Juan Garrido-Salgado

lent me a couple of books
by Roque Dalton
and Ernesto Cardenal

I read them on the bus
on my way into work

and then in my office
while I drank coffee

I read them
sitting in the park
and later in my lounge room
over a glass of red

until worn out
by revolution
I fell asleep
on the couch

only to be woken
by the phone

a voice
reached me
through shadows
and static of the tv

stretched and broken
I hardly recognised
my friend
the poet
with news from Chile

los pacos mataron a mi amigo
la injusticia sigue

the cops killed my friend
the injustice doesn't stop

Chris

I barely recognise you
sitting in a bus shelter
at Flinders Medical Centre
sucking on a Horizon cigarette
blood splattered over bare feet
blood-stained bandages on both wrists
and one over the arterial vein
in your neck

at first I think
you've tried to end it

then you tell me
about the 48 hours
in intensive care
a tube down your throat
into your stomach
one up your arse
another in your dick
the heavy sedation

how you pissed blood
that morning

back in the ward
the nurse carries out
two-hourly obs

I'm caught by surprise
as you slowly recite
your name and date of birth
as though we're back in class
you come in a month younger

your wife
tells me
how she found you
and fears
next time
might be the last

while your daughter
sits on the bed smiling
watching cartoons
on the hospital tv

2
six months later
I visit you
in a city backpackers

you've become a tourist
in your own town

I tell you
you can make it through
the next few weeks
until you're booked
into rehab

you say
we'll see
and show me
how long
a few weeks
can be

3
I guess
it's the small things

the feeling
of rain
on my flesh
on a cold day

or the surprise
of sunshine
when clouds break

or the relief
and earthy smell
of rain
a change of weather
can bring

or the pleasure
of eating
roast chicken

all this
imbued with the after glow
of your passing.

Vanishing point

for Syd Harrex, 1934–2015

life is lived
between the asylum
and the grave

you revealed
in the afternoon light
over lunch
and bottles
of chardonnay

I had thought of death
as a vertical line
something to journey toward
not this horizontal crab shuffle

a change in perspective
not unlike when
with a flourish of hand
you upturned a wine glass
and exclaimed
this is what the poem must do!

I now recognise
table 10 regulars
through Proustian guise
at your funeral

it's as though
you've brought us all
a step closer
to the grave

while later
down the road
on the pub veranda
we up-end our glasses
in a final salute
as your parade
rolls by

and the asylum
slips over the horizon.

Humble wine

it's a light night
the full moon
sits low in the east
lights my path
and reminds me of poems
by Bai Juyi
a book my father lent me
so direct and clear
his words from 1200 years ago
could have been written
yesterday

I think of my father's
humble wine and
his late friends
a distance as great as it was
in Bai Juyi's time
no letter can breach

to the west
a valley
where they are creating
wetlands
over 10,000 seedlings planted
their protective casings
glowing in the moonlight

will he live
to see them blossom?

Coming Home to Roost

My father had an aged care assessment.
He'd been in hospital for a couple of weeks
following another heart attack.
I prepped him beforehand
told him to make a good impression
so they would let him come home. He's hard
of hearing and we helped with interpreting
as the assessor ran through something called
The Transition Care Program. My two sisters
came in and out of the room making sure
he understood. The assessment lasted a couple of hours
my father nodded and signed various papers.
We spoke in loud deep voices to repeat what
the transition care nurse was saying. After the interview
my father was alone in his room with my older sister.
He turned to her and asked *who's going home?*
The chooks?

Dou Dou

I take my father's dog
for a walk on the beach
and think of One Petal
chasing her dog Dou Dou down the street.
They would make a great couple
Dou Dou and my father
one blind the other deaf.
My father's goals are reduced
to walking his dog again one day.
I take her off the leash and watch her run
to the water's edge.

Portrait of my wife's 114-year-old great grandfather

he raised the twisted fingers
of his right hand
to his forehead
where they rested
beneath the brim
of a black beret

he stared at us
through the fog and shadows
of the past century
his eye balls pushing
against the yellow glass
of black-framed spectacles
that rode the wrinkled
sun-spotted flesh
above his ears

the left hand
assumed its cupped position
behind his good ear
while his shrunken lips
opened and closed
mimicking conversation
and occasionally revealing
a single, rotted tooth
jutting forth
from the bottom gum

breaking his silence
on occasion
with a sudden
high-pitched
gracias mi hija!
for a cup of tea
or some food
or whatever it was
his elderly daughter
placed before him

On justice & jazz

higher than the 17th floor
where I write & research justice

lower than the tragedy
of children with disabilities
preyed on by paedophiles
while parents are denied justice

& the broken
men & women
with brain injuries
& mental illness
who fill our jails
& institutions

faster than the drop
of the lift
as though we're all contained
in this one architecture
of pain

exceeding the heights
& depths of it

only this trumpet
here & now.

Section Five

Post apocalypse

Wednesday 28 November 2016, Adelaide

the day of the storm
I had a poetry reading
with Nathan Curnow
overland from Ballarat
to launch his collection
The Apocalypse Awards
an hour into the unprecedented
state-wide blackout
I took his call

you bastard
you brought the apocalypse with you
the reading cancelled
I waited around in the darkness
still in the office
with a swag of poetry books
and no way to get home
on the electric train
the city in gridlock

the rain stopped
I ventured into the half light
people wandered the streets
with fear on their faces
and nervous laughter
cars bumper to bumper

I decided I'd walk to my father's
an hour north of the city
I passed a huddle of Ministers
scheming down the steps of Parliament House
toward the intersection
of King William St and North Tce
where bystanders stood transfixed
watching a fire truck
stuck in the middle of the intersection
sirens wailing
a man in high viz gear
consulted with the driver
and eventually the truck
negotiated a way through

the politicians stood there
with blank faces
some partially shielded by their advisors' umbrellas
guys I'd written dozens of speeches for
powerless now
like the rest of us

I walked towards North Adelaide
most of the shops were closed
I realised I had no cash
the Oxford had a hand written sign
on the door of the front bar
in blue pen
open til 6 pm
inside a few punters
nursed beers by candle light

I walked on past the banked up traffic
feeling the weight of poetry books
on my back
their ink would outlast
the electronic readers
though even libraries burn

I felt hungry
and wondered if my father
had food in his house
he'd have long-life milk
tinned food and cash
I was a teenager again
lobbing at his door
broke and hungry
tired from the walk
how much longer
will I have this refuge?

six months ago
I held his hand
while he lay sedated
for four days
following a triple by-pass
when they finally roused him
he asked me if he was married
and I had to break the news
not once but twice
and twice divorced
our roles reversed

as he pieced together his life
and I answered the big questions
like how we came to be here

as the days passed the fog cleared
and here I was now at his door
the dog barking

that'll teach the stupid bastards
to close Port Augusta Power Station
we'd driven by it the year before
observed the stream of smoke
rising from the stack
and he'd posed the question then
how that thin trail of emissions
in so much space
could impact on the atmosphere

and now I see his carbon-based world view
vindicated as the batteries on my phone
run down and before long
the device is useless
while on my wrist
the LED lights of my smart watch
flash wastefully in the candle light
as my father discourses
on candle power
and how they used to have
six candles at each end of the table

he tells me
the smell of burning wax
brings back memories of the block
on Maize Island in the Riverland
while for me the blue kerosene lantern
brings back memories of my own childhood
camping on the block
amidst the ruins
of his ancestral home

and I guess all the old timers
will be thinking of the '56 flood
I remember him telling me
as a child
it would happen again
but I couldn't imagine the Torrens River
ever bursting its banks
and now the dams and reservoirs
are full and the Torrens gushes past the weir

I'm in the right place to survive the apocalypse
my father's world of hand tools
his brace and bit with assorted augers
rip saws and other tools
he's never owned a power tool
we haven't had a blackout this good
in a long time
he exclaims happily
and for once isn't alone with the tv

we suck on cask wine
I pull out my new chapbook

and finally get to show him the poems
he takes his time reading the book
and I wonder why I haven't found time
to share some of the poems
over two years old now
we hold our own slow reading
in the candle light
my swag of books not wasted

a few hours later
I borrow his VS Commodore
to drive home through
the windswept darkness
negotiating intersections
without any fear of breathos

when I hit the southern suburbs
order is restored
the lights are back on
as the grid is built up
suburb by suburb

I'm re-united with my family
impressed by their resourcefulness

and by morning
I'm awake to both sides of politics
working the airwaves
renewables vs energy security
Turnbull stoking the coalfires
Weatherill weathering the storm.

The sun and the moon

in the front bar
a man with a sun
tattooed on his forearm
gesticulates wildly
to the bar staff

I order my beer
take a sip
and sit quietly on my stool
a lonely old moon
with pockets for craters

Alfajor

We eat alfajores
and membrillo
from Argentina
bought in Melbourne.
There's no translation
for alfajor.
You'll find dulce de leche
inside.
There's no real translation for that
either
although caramel comes close.
The alfajor is round
with biscuit on the outside.
Individually wrapped
they taste as good
as the word alfajor.
Pronounce the j like an h
as though your mouth is full
of sweetness.

Zucchini flowers

I meet Sergio
at the café
we talk about poetry
as we eat
three zucchini flowers
home-cooked
Italian style
covered in a light
egg batter
a small sun inside each one

When she washes her hair

for Angie

When she washes her hair
the brush lies quietly in its drawer
a breeze turns the pages of an open book
ink on parchment dries
tea leaves swell and cool in the pot.
May the faucets open and hot water sing
while the world awaits
the subtle perfume of her hair.

Acknowledgements

For first publication of poems in this book, grateful acknowledgement is made to the following: *Antipodes, Australian Book Review, Communion, Huawen Wenxue: A Bilingual Selection of Poetry in Chinese and English, Just off Message Anthology, Poetry NZ, Radio Adelaide, Social Alternatives, Transnational Literature* and *Quadrant*. Poems from the collection were also published in Spanish translation in *Alhucema* (Spain) and *Estudio M5* (Chile), and in Chinese translation in 散文诗世界 (*The World of Prose Poetry*). Some of the poems appeared in the chapbook *Jardin du Luxembourg* (Garron Publishing 2016).

Many thanks to Graham Rowlands for editing the manuscript and ordering the poems.

Printed in Australia
AUHW011926121120
336963AU00002B/2